Berthold Seemann

History of the Isthmus of Panama

Berthold Seemann

History of the Isthmus of Panama

ISBN/EAN: 9783743401310

Manufactured in Europe, USA, Canada, Australia, Japa

Cover: Foto ©ninafisch / pixelio.de

Manufactured and distributed by brebook publishing software
(www.brebook.com)

Berthold Seemann

History of the Isthmus of Panama

HISTORY

OF THE

ISTHMUS OF PANAMA,

BY

𝔇𝔯. 𝔅𝔢𝔯𝔱𝔥𝔬𝔩𝔡 𝔖𝔢𝔢𝔪𝔞𝔫𝔫.

PRINTED & PUBLISHED AT THE OFFICE OF THE STAR & HERALD,

PANAMA, 1867.

INTRODUCTION.

In the little work which we now place before our readers we make no pretentions to publishing a full history of the Isthmus of Panama, but merely to give an outline of the most exciting events which occurred in the early part of its settlement, embracing the invasion and capture of Portobello and Old Panama by the Buccaneers. In fact the work is merely a series of notes from the able pen of the well known traveller and author, DR. BERTHOLD SEEMANN, thrown loosely together some twenty years ago, with a view to publish them in a complete form at some future day. More important matters, however, have since then occupied the author's attention, and he has, at our special request, handed the notes over to us in their crude state to make such use as we pleased of them. Any alterations we might make in them would only detract from their merit, so we give them to the public as they were given to us. A further series of these notes from the period where these end to a very recent date have been promised us by DR. SEEMANN, on his return home from his present excursion to Central America, which we intend issuing as a continuation of and in a style similar to the present publication, as soon as they reach us.

THE PUBLISHERS.

PANAMA, DECEMBER, 1866.

HISTORY

OF THE

ISTHMUS OF PANAMA.

The treasure constantly conveyed across the Isthmus by the Spaniards did not escape the vigilant eyes of the pirates, who toward the middle of the 16th century, were already getting numerous in the Caribbean Sea. The Galleons were too well armed to suffer an attack to be made on them with impunity. Other schemes had therefore to be resorted to. In 1572 the *Planché* and *Swan* were fitted out in England, and the command given to Francis Drake and his brothers. The object of this expedition was to intercept a treasure of great value which was said to be carried from Panama to Nombre de Dios. Drake being joined on the coast of South America by another bark, landed at Nombre de Dios, dismounted the guns of the platform, and while the alarm-bells were ringing and drums beating, marched to the market place. Here a desperate fight ensued, in which Drake received a wound, but knowing that if the general's heart stoops the men's will fail, he concealed it. One of his trusty followers, Oxenham, and his brother, with sixteen men, proceeded to the King's treasure house, and here piles of silver were found, and still more in the Governor's residence. Drake then told his men that " he had brought them to the treasury of the world, and if they did not gain it, none but themselves were to blame." Here, however, from loss of blood his strength failed him. His men bound up the wound and carried him by main force to his pinnace.

On recovering, Drake decided on crossing the Isthmus ; but having lost many men by sickness, among them his brothers Joseph and John, he removed the remaining force to his own ship and pinnace. The *Swan* was sunk. His object was to intercept on the Isthmus, a train of mules, laden with the King's treasure. On meeting it he attacked and chased the party in charge, as far as Cruces, giving strict orders to his company not to hurt women or unarmed men. In their wanderings they came to a high tree, and climbing it viewed with transports of joy the great Pacific, an Ocean as yet entirely closed to English enterprise.

Among those who accompanied Drake was one John Oxman, or Oxenham, who appears to have been a favorite with the captain, and who shortly afterwards returned to try his fortune in a hazardous scheme of privateering. In 1575, he arrived on the Atlantic side of the Isthmus, in a vessel of 140 tons, and with only 70 men. Hearing that, since the attempt of Drake, the treasure of the Spaniards was strongly guarded, he devised a scheme of action equally bold and original. Drawing the ship on shore, he covered her with boughs of trees, buried the guns, except two small pieces, and leaving one man as a watch, he marched with the rest into the interior. He soon arrived at a river flowing towards the south. Here he built a pinnace 45 feet in length, and in her went down stream into the South Sea. Directing his course to the Pearl Islands, he captured a bark containing 60,000 pesos of gold, and another from Lima with 100,000 pesos of silver. Not satisfied yet he proceeded to the Islands where pearls are mostly found. Having collected a small quantity, he set off with his pinnace and his prizes to the mouth of the river which he had descended, and having dismissed the two captured vessels, began to ascend it. The delay of fifteen days on the Pearl Islands was fatal to him. The very night that he left those islands the negroes set off for Panama to give information of what had happened. Four barks, each with 25 armed men, besides negroes to row them, under the command of Juan de Ortega, were immediately sent in search of Oxenham. They fell in with the prizes which Oxenham had dismissed, and learnt from them the course which the pirates had taken. After rowing several days against the stream, they arrived at the place where the treasure had been provisionally buried. This they hastened to carry off, well satisfied with their success. The English, returning to the spot and finding the treasure gone, followed with impetuosity, and regardless of the inequality of numbers. The consequence was that they fell into an ambush and were totally defeated. A party of Spaniards soon after discovered Oxenham's ship, with the stores and ordnance, which he had taken such pains to conceal. The English who survived this train of misfortunes lived for some time among the Darien Indians, employed in building canoes, in which they hoped to effect their escape. But at length they were taken by the Spaniards and carried to Panama, where Oxenham and his companions, with the exception of five boys, were put to death. Thus ended the first Englishmen who navigated the Pacific. (1.)

Drake after his famous voyage round the world, was employed by Queen Elizabeth against Philip II. In 1595, the Queen fitted out an expedition destined to strike a blow at the power of Spain, by attacking the West Indies. The armament, consisting of six ships, was unfortunate. Sir John Hawkins, one of the

(1.) Lardner, History of Maritime and Inland discovery. Vol. II. p. 248.

commanders, died ; Drake's smallest ship was taken by the Spaniards, who, by putting her crew to the torture, extracted information respecting the plans of the expedition, and when Drake attacked Porto Rico he found the place fully warned. Sailing away he took and burnt Riohacha, Ranchera, Santa Marta and Nombre de Dios, getting no greater spoil than twenty tons of silver and two bars of gold. Whilst Drake remained in the harbor of Nombre de Dios, Sir Thomas Baskerville, with a part of the land forces, made an attempt to cross the Isthmus and destroy the City of Panama. But a fatal disease broke out among the soldiers and sailors, and deprived them of the services of their chief surgeon. When many of his men and three of his captains had died, the hardy Drake himself fell sick, and after struggling some twenty days with his malady and the grief occasioned by his failures, he expired on the 28th of December, 1595. On the same day the fleet anchored off Portobello, and in sight of the place which he had formerly taken and plundered, his body received a sailor's funeral. (2.)

The bold attempts of Oxenham and Drake filled the Isthmenians with apprehension, and prompted them to adopt a more regular system of defence than their fancied security hitherto seemed to demand. Little did they anticipate that these events were only the prelude to a fearful tragedy of which their country was to become the theatre. The principal actors in this tragedy, whose names for nearly a century were the terror of the coast and the scourge of the sea, were the Buccaneers, an association equally singular and formidable, and called into existence by the despotic administration of the Spanish colonies. The Spaniards themselves felt oppressed by the restrictions placed on trade,

(2.) Barrow, p. 141-143.

and gave stealthy encouragement to foreign interlopers, who supplied them at an easier rate with articles which could not be legally procured without paying enormous exactions. English traders soon made their appearance; and, as the authorities on the one hand treated them as enemies, or even as pirates, while on the other they were invited by the profits of a contraband trade, they soon learned to adopt the precaution of going well armed. (3.)

The cruelties of the Spaniards to the aborigines of Cuba terminated in the depopulation of that fine Island. The cattle at the same time multiplied in great numbers, and roved over the deserted tracts of the western districts. This, in consequence, became the victualling place of all foreign vessels that cruised upon the Spanish Main or disturbed its trade. The preparation of the meat became a regular business. Spanish hunters killed the cattle ; the flesh was then dried and prepared according to the Carib method, on hurdles raised a few feet above the fire. This mode of dressing food was called by the Indians " boocan," a name also applied to the apparatus used in the process, and to the meat itself. Hence the persons who were employed in procuring provisions for the cruisers, adopting the language with the habits of the natives, called themselves Buccaneers.

A large majority of these adventurers were English ; and as their smuggling trade quickly degenerated into actual piracy, they took the honourable designation of freebooters. There was a natural alliance between the freebooters and Buccaneers; they mutually depended on one another, the avocations of one party being at sea, those of the other on land. It is probable that in some instances the pirate cured his own provisions, and so united both professions in his own person. But in general the hunters were

_____

(3) Lardner. History of Maritime and Inland Discovery, chap. 19.

distinct from the seamen, and in process of time, a majority of the
hunters were French, while the rovers were chiefly English. Yet
the adventurers of these two nations whimsically thought fit to
borrow the name of their profession from the language of the
other, as if the respectability of their calling could be enhanced,
or its criminality palliated by a foreign name. The English called
themselves Buccaneers, while the French preferred the title of
Freebooters, or corruptedly, Filibusters.

All the adventurers, of whatever nation, made the Spaniards
the sole object of attack. A sense of common interest bound them
together and formed them into a society styling itself: *The
brethren of the Coast.* The Buccaneers had peculiar customs, which
either from necessity or tradition obtained the authority of law.
Their code of morality was such as might be expected among men
who, while they renounced a friendly intercourse with the rest of
mankind, depended upon each other's fidelity. Every Buccaneer
had a mate, who was the heir to all his money. In some instances a community of property existed. Negligence of dress,
and even dirtiness, was prescribed by their fashions, as best befit-
ting a desperado. But when, in case of war between their nations and the Spaniards, they could obtain commissions, they were
always ready to take the name of privateers. (4)

The increase of the Buccaneers was regarded with satisfaction
by other European States. They reasoned with the laxity of
political morality then prevailing, that they might profit by illegal
proceedings, which at the same time they were not called upon to
avow. Various settlements were made by adventurers through-
out the West India Islands, those of the same nation generally
associating together; and as they grew into importance, they were

(4) Lardner, ibid.

claimed by that crown of which a majority of the colonists were subjects. The pirates were pleased to find themselves countenanced or connived at by legal governments, and colonies offered a prospect of an increased market for their trade. Becoming more confident in their strength, they seized on the little island of Tortuga. This was the first step of the Buccaneers towards forming themselves into an independent society. The severity of the Spaniards soon after forced them to take one of still greater importance. A party of Spanish troops surprised Tortuga, while most of the Buccaneers were hunting on the main land, or cruising in their vessels, and those surprised were hanged as pirates without mercy or distinction. But national animosity and the love of gain have more influence than terror, and the ranks of the Buccaneers, after their loss of Tortuga, were speedily recruited. From this blow they learnt the necessity of observing more regularity in their proceedings ; and for the first time, they elected a commander. As they acknowledged no claims to rank but conduct and courage, all their leaders were remarkable for personal prowess and daring exploits, but they never felt the compunctions of humanity, and cruelties stained the glory of their successes (1.)

Among the most notorious and fortunate of these leaders ranks Henry Morgan, under whose government the affairs of the Buccaneers obtained their most flourishing condition. Morgan was born in Wales of respectable parents. His father was a farmer, but young Morgan showed little inclination to follow his peaceful calling. At an early age he left home to seek employment more suited to his active mind, and arriving at one of the seaports, joined a vessel bound for Barbadoes. No sooner, however, had

(1) Lardner—ibid.

the destination been reached than according to the practice of those times, Morgan was sold as a slave, and had to serve a series of years in that capacity. Having at last regained his freedom, he proceeded to Jamaica to try his fortune once more. There he found two piratical vessels ready for sea, and being without employment, he did not hesitate to join them. A new career was now opened to him. He soon acquired their manners and customs, and having, during several successful voyages, saved a little money, he agreed with some of his associates to join stock and buy a ship. This was quickly executed and Morgan chosen commander. He directed his course towards the coast of Campeachy, and returned to Jamaica with several captured vessels. Mansvelt, an old pirate, seeing Morgan in possession of such valuable prizes, formed a high idea of his piratical talents, and offered him the command of Vice-Admiral of a fleet, consisting of fifteen sail and five hundred men, which he was fitting out, and which was destined to invade the American continent. Morgan accepted the offer and made himself prominent in the new situation. He took several places, and after the death of Mansvelt, the office of Commander-in-chief, was unanimously conferred upon him.

His exploits after this installation were of the boldest character. With a body of seven hundred men, he took the town of Puerto del Principe in Cuba. His next undertaking was directed against Portobello. He had only four hundred and sixty men ; but his advance was so rapid, that he came on the town by surprise, and found it quite unprepared. In storming the castle, he compelled his prisoners, chiefly religious of both sexes, to apply the scaling-ladders to the walls. When the garrison surrendered, he shut them up in the castle, and setting fire to the magazine, destroyed the fort and its defenders together. He afterwards sacked Maracaibo, and the neighboring town of Gibraltar; and, emboldened by success, he consulted with his officers which of the three places, Carthagena, Veracruz or Panama, he should next attack. Panama was believed to be the richest, and on that city the lot fell.

The opinion of the Buccaneers was, that it would be most expeditious to invade the Isthmus by ascending the river Chagres, as far as Cruces, and thence proceed by land to Panama. Yet even this plan, the most feasible that could be devised, was attended with difficulties. The mouth of the river was guarded by the Castle of San Lorenzo, which stood on a high rock the top of which had been divided by a ditch into two parts. Palisades filled with earth, encircled the building; a drawbridge formed its only entrance. Towards the land it had four bastions, towards the sea, two; the southern side was rendered inaccessible by the steepness of the rock, the northern, by the bed of the river; while the foot, protected by a battery, commanded the mouth of the Chagres, which possessed besides the defence of a hidden rock. The garrison, consisting of three hundred and fourteen men, was well armed and prepared for an attack by previous notice.

Morgan would have proceeded in person to commence operations, but he was engaged in the Island of Santa Catalina. To lose no time he sent four ships, a boat and four hundred men, under the command of Captain Brodely, to clear the way for the main forces. No sooner did this flotilla arrive in sight of the Castle than the Spaniards opened fire so well directed and kept up with so much spirit, that the pirates were obliged to take refuge in a small bay, about a league distant. Men less accustomed to hazardous undertakings would, probably, have deferred assaulting a place so well defended; but the Buccaneers, however discouraged, were ready to make a formal attack. Landing early on the next morning, they forced a passage through the forest, and reached the Castle about two o'clock in the afternoon. Notwithstanding that they had been covered by trees, their movements had been watched, and they had hardly approached within a cannon shot, when a fire was opened upon them, killing several of their number before the assault could be made. However they continued to advance, holding the sword in one hand, the fireball in the other. But the garrison defended itself so well, that the design to climb the walls and set fire to the palisades failed, and retreat became inevitable.

This repulse did not shake their resolution. At nightfall another assault was made. As before their aim was to fire the palisades; but they would probably have met with no more success than on the former occasion, had not an accident come to their assistance. In the height of the tumult a part of the building became ignited. All eyes being turned towards the assailants, it remained unnoticed until reaching a barrel of gunpowder. The explosion that followed produced the utmost consternation within the walls, and, water being wanting, the flames spread with rapidity, illuminating the scene of destruction, and shewing to the trembling garrison the savage faces of the pirates. The latter had taken advantage of the confusion by setting fire to the palisades; they now tried to climb the walls, but the Spaniards, anticipating this movement, threw down pots filled with combustible matter and, fighting with bravery, succeeded for a while in checking the progress of the invaders. Yet, in spite of all their efforts they continued to lose ground, and their numbers were rapidly dwindling away. At day-break the fortress was a mere ruin ; the flames had made several breaches, earth had fallen into the ditch, and thus removed one of the greatest obstacles to the entry into the fort. Meanwhile the fighting was kept up, and about noon the English gained a breach which was defended by twenty-five men, headed by the Governor in person. A desperate struggle ensued. The Governor collecting all his men and disdaining any quarter, fought till a musket shot laid him low. Resistance was now at an end, the remainder of the garrison either escaped or precipitated themselves into the sea ; and out of a body of three hundred and fourteen men, only thirty were made prisoners.

This victory had been dearly purchased. The pirates had one hundred killed and seventy wounded. From the prisoners it was learnt that the Governor of Panama had received notice of their intended invasion about three weeks previously, and that in consequence of this information, he had sent one hundred and sixty-four men to strengthen San Lorenzo, placed ambuscades on the banks of the Chagres, and collected two thousand six hundred men on the plains of Panama to repulse, if necessary, any attack on the capital. A vessel was immediately dispatched to acquaint the Admiral of the Buccaneers with the success and the information extracted. Shortly after the whole piratical fleet hove in sight, and great was the rejoicing on board when the English colours were seen waving from San Lorenzo, a castle hitherto deemed impregnable. The eagerness of the ships, however, to get into the river proved disastrous. Unacquainted with the sunken rocks at its entrance, four, among them that of Morgan, grounded, and the crews with difficulty saved their lives.

The arrival of the fleet gave a fresh impulse to the execution of the invaders' plans. By compelling the Spanish prisoners to work, and by their own exertions, the castle was restored as well as possible; five hundred men were left for its defence, and the coasting vessels which still remained in the river, and usually carried two or three guns, were seized; in fine, every precaution was taken to secure a safe retreat. On the 18th of January, 1671, all necessary arrangements were completed, and on that day Morgan embarked with one thousand two hundred men, in five boats and thirty two canoes.

In ascending the river Chagres many impediments presented themselves, a rapid current, a want of practice in managing the flat bottomed and overloaded canoes, and the utmost scarcity of provisions. The ambuscades placed on the banks, which Morgan intended to surprise and plunder of their provisions, having been seized by the general terror which the fall of San Lorenzo had produced, had abandoned their position before the Buccaneers reached them, and left nothing save their traces behind. Exhausted with fatigue, and tormented by hunger, six days had already been spent without reaching Cruces, a village which under ordinary circumstances may be gained in thirty-six hours. Many began to murmur and to curse the day when engaging in an undertaking which they now deemed beyond their power to accomplish. Morgan, however, backed by a large majority, succeeded in quelling the discontent, and tried to exhilarate their spirits by brilliant promises of future gain and immediate prospects of plenty on arriving at Cruces.

At last Cruces was reached, but how great was the disappointment on finding most of the houses in flames, the inhabitants fled and, except sixteen jars of Peruvian wine, a bag full of bread, and several cats and dogs, provisions of every kind removed. The march to Panama was, therefore, pushed on with greater eagerness. After the canoes and boats had been sent some distance down the river to prevent their being taken by the Spaniards, the Buccaneers entered the forest which stretched from Cruces to the plains of Panama. The Isthmenians had taken advantage of its thickness, by placing in different parts Indians who, armed with bows, arrows and javelins, attacked the invaders on various occasions.

In spite of every impediment the march was continued, and on the ninth day after departing from Chagres, the first sight of the South sea was obtained. After being so long among the darkness and monotony of primeval forests, the grandeur of the scene thus suddenly opening made even on the minds of the Buccaneers a favorable impression. Before them rolled the Pacific Ocean, enlivened by ships, and the delightful group of islands justly termed the garden of Panama ; and around them stretched plains with groves of gay-flowering trees and shrubs, numerous herds of cattle roving among them. The landscape was so enchanting that all broke out in loud acclamations; and when towards evening the steeples of Panama were descried, the joy reached the highest pitch. Drums were beaten, guns discharged, trumpets sounded and, as if victory had already been obtained, a general content prevailed. After the camp had been pitched, bullocks were roasted, all fatigue seemed to be forgotten, and for the first time since the commencement of the invasion, sound sleep—undisturbed by the bodies of soldiers who occasionally appeared to watch their movements—visited their exhausted frames.

The city of Panama was at that period about four miles eastward of the present site. The traveller still finds the ruins of that once opulent place, though almost hid by a luxuriant vegetation; he still meets the remains of several public buildings, the tower of the Cathedral, the walls of the churches, bridges, turrets, cisterns, and partly the pavement of the streets, all overrun by huge fig-trees, pepper-bushes and numerous creepers whose flowers perfume the air with fragrance. But in vain does he seek for the enterprising community from which Pizarro drew his most daring followers for the conquest of Peru. The spot is deserted. Unhealthy exhalations and noxious insects prevent any human being from inhabiting it, and Pumas, Iguanas, Alligators and Snakes now occupy the places where formerly the conquest of an Empire was planned.

On the day previous to Morgan's assault Panama presented a different aspect. Seven thousand houses, composed of the precious woods in which the country abounds, formed several stately streets. Two thousand of the buildings, historians tell us, were truly magnificent; fine paintings adorned the walls, costly hangings the balconies and verandas. Eight monastaries—seven of which were inhabited by monks, one by nuns—arose in different parts. The two churches were richly ornamented; altar pieces from the hands of the first artists and gold and silver vessels decorated their interior. A hospital afforded shelter to the sick; the Genoese also, had a stately house for their trade of negroes; and numerous stables existed for the beasts that carried the King's silver to Cruces and Portobello, or served for other commercial purposes. Nor had the defence of the city been forgotten. Towards the land the place was protected by strong fortifications, and towards the sea its situation was such that, on account of the shoal-water which left at ebb tide nearly for two miles nothing save bare rocks, no vessel could approach it. The vicinity was converted into plantations and gardens, in which the fair Panamenians enjoyed the freshness of the morning, or partook of the cooling breezes of the tropical evening. The inhabitants were mostly merchants who employed a vast number of slaves. Many skilful mechanics and artizans, encouraged by a ready market at the time of the Porto Bello fair, and a number of opulent citizens, had taken up their residence here. Panama, being besides the See of a Bishop and the site of the Provincial Government, contained many ecclesiastical and civil officers, with their usual train of attendants. It was this city which a few boats' crews dared to attack! which was to fall before a handful of pirates!

A faint purple had hardly announced the dawn of the 27th of January, 1671—the last day which the devoted place, after a short but brilliant existance of 152 years, was to witness—when the drums and trumpets called the Buccaneers to the attack, and made them conscious that the time had arrived when they must either defeat their enemies, or fall themselves victims to their own daring plans. Adopting the advice of the guides they avoided the direct road leading to the city on which ample preparations had been made for their repulse, and took another which traversed a wood, and though being very irksome and difficult to pass, had the advantage of conducting them out of the reach of the ambuscades and batteries.

When daylight was fully established they found themselves on a little hill, still known by the name of "Cerro de Advance," from the top of which they perceived the full extent of the forces they had to contend with. The Spaniards were arranged in battle array, and their forces consisted of two squadrons of horse and four regiments of foot; they had besides a number of wild bullocks, driven by Indians and negroes, by which odd addition they hoped to destroy an enemy whom they fancied ignorant of bull-fighting. The Buccaneers, surprised at beholding a force so much superior to their own, would instantly have relinquished all thoughts of attack had an alternative been left them.   But there was no choice.   Dividing themselves into three batallions, two hundred men, the most skillful at their guns were sent as an advance guard, whilst the main body descended the hill, marching straight towards the enemy.   These movements were the mutual signal for action.   The Spaniards, shouting "Viva el Rey," immediately pushed forward their cavalry, accompanied by some of the foot regiments; but, before they had time to inflict any injury the advanced guard discharged upon them a volley of musketry.   The fighting now became general, and both sides displayed the utmost courage; the Spaniards, however, soon perceived that they had no longer naked Indians to contend with, that, on the contrary, their opponents belonged to a race superior to themselves.

After two hours hard fighting the Panamenians began to waver; their cavalry could not act advantageously on the boggy ground, and most of the horsemen were killed.   Finding themselves baffled in this manner they had recourse to the bullocks, driving them from behind to create confusion, but the wild cattle frightened by the unwonted noise, mostly ran away, and the few that broke through the lines of the Buccaneers were easily slain. The horsemen were the first who fled from the field; they were soon followed, however, by the infantry, who, seeing their companions deserting them, discharged their muskets, threw down their arms and seconded them in their cowardice.   Those that were not so fortunate as to effect their escape hid themselves among the mangroves, where, when discovered, they were killed without mercy.   Six thousand Spaniards were dyeing the savannas with their blood, and a considerable number of the pirates shared the same fate.

The great prize lay now within grasp, it was necessary to seize it before additional forces could withhold it. Morgan, elated by success, ordered an instant assault on the city, and without any loss of time, the infuriated multitude advanced towards the gates. The combat now became terrible; one party fighting for the possession of those golden treasures which had always been the fame of the country, and the envy of foreigners, the other defending their homes, their wives, their children, all that was dear to them. The Panamenians displayed a heroism rivalling that of the ancient Spartans, but considerable as was the havoc which their grape and musket shots occasioned, great as was the number of assailants that fell, the resolution of the Buccaneers was not to be shaken, on the contrary, their eagerness seemed to increase in proportion as their losses augmented. At last, after three hours of close combat, the citizens were vanquished, and their conquerors entered triumphantly the "Golden Cup," the object of all their toil and exertion.

Thus fell Panama, in those days one of the most opulent cities on the American continent. It did not fall before an army, backed by the power and influence of a great nation, but before a band of adventurers, the mere scum of European society. Could at that moment the old Panamenians have risen from their graves, they would have uttered a cry of distress on beholding their offspring praying for mercy at the feet of a set of rovers. Many of the citizens were only the grand-children of those men whose bravery, perseverance and fortitude explored the boundless shores of the Pacific Ocean, the grand-children of those men who overran Central America, Veraguas and Darien, and added the empires of Quito, Peru and Chile to the dominions of the Spanish crown.

. After the confusion had abated, Morgan assembled his men, and knowing their propensity of indulging too freely in the use of intoxicating beverages after a victory, he pretended to have received information that poison had been introduced into the cellars. The pretence was so plausible that it served its purpose; preventing debauchery which must have proved their inevitable ruin, when considerable bodies of the enemy were still in the neighbourhood and ready to take advantage of any neglect on the part of their foes, in order to renew the attack and recapture the city. Panama was now formally ransacked. It was found to contain great warehouses, well stored with all kinds of valuable merchandize, but as these articles were generally too bulky to be much appreciated, the Buccaneers looked more for the precious metals which could be conveyed across the country with comparative ease. In this respect, however, they were greviously disappointed ; the ornaments of the churckes and convents, the King's plate and jewels, as well as most other valuables, had been placed on board a vessel, which, though badly provisioned, and with only one sail on the main-mast, had effected its escape. The intelligence had hardly been communicated to Morgan, when he sent a large boat with twenty-five men, entreating them to use every means in their power to overtake so valuable a prize.

The Panamenians had hitherto little felt the consequences of their defeat, but they were to drain the cup of bitterness to the very bottom. Morgan gave, privately, orders to set fire to the principal buildings ; the flames, aided by a strong breeze, soon spread about and consumed a whole street in an hour. The inhabitants as well as the pirates, who were mostly ignorant of the real origin of the fire, tried to quench it by pulling down houses or blowing them up with gunpowder. All was of no avail.

Before night the greater portion of Panama was reduced to ashes, and nothing remained of the beautiful city save a heap of smoking ruins. Morgan, when accused by his followers of this impolitic atrocity, pointed to the Spaniards as the originators. This assertion, however, found no credit. He delighted in any thing cruel, and had probably no other motive for his incendiary act than Nero had when he wanted to enjoy the sight of a great conflagration.

Most of the Buccaneers were still encamped outside the walls, closely united for fear of an attack; but when, after a lapse of several days, they perceived that their opponents were destitute of the necessary courage, they re-entered the city and deposited the sick in the few buildings that had escaped destruction. A careful search was made among the ruins for utensils of plate and gold, by means of which they obtained, especially from the wells and cisterns, considerable quantities. To acquire still more, parties of two hundred men were dispatched into the country. These expeditions were successful, making a considerable number of prisoners, and gathering a great amount of valuables. In order to make the captives confess where the treasures were concealed, they were subjected to the most cruel tortures, the bare recital of which is horror-striking. The poor wretches could seldom stand the diabolical treatment, and many expired under its application.

The twenty-five men sent in pursuit of the rich vessel came back, bringing several prizes. They had failed, however, in the real object of their mission, having given themselves up to debauchery instead of proceeding at once on their voyage, and thus enabled the prize to escape. The rage of Morgan knew no bounds, and he instantly dispatched three other boats to re-

new the search   These cruized several days and visited many
ports and creeks, but met with no success.   Their disappointment,
however, was in some measure relieved by capturing a boat, and
afterward at Taboga a ship just arrived from Payta and laden with
provisions, merchandize and twenty thousand pieces of eight.

A convoy, which had been sent to Chagres to acquaint those
left in charge of the castle with the victory of Panama, returned
about the same time.   The pirates of that place had dispatched
two boats to cruize, which, meeting a Spanish vessel, chased her
in sight of the castle.   The look-out on the tower perceiving the
manœuvre, instantly hoisted Spanish colours.   The stratagem
was successful.   The vessel in seeking refuge under the cannon
of the stronghold, was boarded and plundered.   Her cargo consisted chiefly of provisions, which proved a most welcome and
timely supply, relieving the pirates from all fear of starvation.
This news was joyfully received, and induced Morgan to prolong
his stay.   New excursions were made, and a regular ransom im-
posed on every prisoner; if, after applying the torture, the unfortunate beings proved unable to produce the requisite sum, no
quarter was granted, no sex or condition spared; the old and the
young, men as well as women, all were equally objects of hatred
and cruelty.

More than three weeks had now elapsed since the commencement of the dreadful catastrophe, and the chief began to think
earnestly about his departure, when a plot was discovered which
retarded it for awhile.   In leading the Buccaneers across the
Isthmus, Morgan had opened to them a new field of enterprise.
The great Pacific Ocean, of whose riches they had heard so much,
and whose waters they had never navigated, stretched in all its
majesty before them.   The prospect was so tempting, that a

considerable number contemplated the plan of leaving Morgan, and proceeding to Europe by way of the East Indies. They intended to take the ship lately captured at Taboga, and had already secretly gathered provisions and naval stores, when their proceedings were discovered. Morgan's resolution was instantly taken. He issued orders to cut down the main-mast, and burn it together with all the boats and coasting vessels that had been seized. Thus, a seperation was prevented which must have proved fatal to all engaged in the invasion.

The preparations for the departure were actively resumed. Many of the prisoners received permission to seek for money to ransom themselves, from their relations or friends; the whole of the artillery was spiked, and a strong party sent in search of the Governor, who, it was reported intended to make an attack. It was soon ascertained, however, that though he entertained such an intention, the people under his command, disheartened by their series of misfortunes, had refused to comply with his orders. At last all was in readiness for a start, and on the 24th of February, 1671, the pirates left the still smoking ruins, carrying off six hundred prisoners and one hundred and seventy-five beasts of burden laden with spoil. One party of the pirates marched in the van, another in the rear, and the captives in the centre. When the march commenced nothing was heard save lamentations and shrieks. The women begged on their knees to restore them to liberty, and not take them from their native land, but Morgan remained deaf to their solicitations, and was unmoved by their tears. On arriving at the village of Cruces it was proclaimed that every one who was not ransomed within three days would be transported as a slave to Jamaica. Many were released by their friends and relations, but a great number were not so fortunate, and some of the inhabitants of Cruces were led into hopeless slavery.

After collecting all the rice and Indian corn that could be obtained, the Buccaneers departed from the village on the 5th of March, taking the same route as before, the river Chagres. When nearly half way, Morgan commanded a general halt, and mustering, every one was obliged to take his oath that he had not concealed or appropriated to himself a particle of the spoil. As might have been expected this solemnity proved a mere farce among a community of men whose morality was of so lax a nature. It was, therefore, necessary to have a different mode of investigation. By common consent each company' appointed an inspector, and the chief was the first who submitted himself to their search. The French assisting in the expedition had a great aversion to these proceedings, and loudly protested against it; but forming the minority they had to submit. After the search was completed all re-embarked and arrived at Chagres on the 9th of March.

A boat was sent to Portobello to ask the Spanish authorities for a ransom of the Castle of San Lorenzo. Their answer however, as had been anticipated, was that Morgan might do whatever he pleased, they would not give a single real for the place. It was accordingly razed to the ground, and, there being no further prospect of booty, the spoil was divided. This proceeding gave rise to much disappointment; instead of the golden treasures which the men expected to obtain, each. after all the toil and danger, received only the scanty sum of two hundred pieces of eight; the rest Morgan kept for himself. The whole community was exasperated in the highest degree, and loudly demanded proper share; no sooner, however, did Morgan see difficulties arising than he

slipped his cable, and accompanied by four other ships, his ac-
complices in the fraud escaped to Jamaica. The indignation of
the fleet knew no bounds on finding themselves deserted, cheated
in the grossest manner, and unprovided with every necessary for
the continuation of the voyage.

With this act Morgan seems to have concluded his piratical
career. He was, undoubtedly, a man who not only displayed
infinite bravery, but the highest qualities of a great commander;
unhappily, however, like most of his predecessors, he was cruel,
blood-thirsty and treacherous. He was afterwards knighted by
Charles II., and became successively Commissioner of the Ad-
miralty Court in Jamaica, and Deputy Governor of that Island.
The elevation of the ruffian to these high posts has been censured,
and called an unwise act. They were far from being so. England,
at that period, began to perceive the full danger of her policy
towards the Buccaneers, and became sensible that it was high
time to put a stop to their proceedings. Their suppression, however, was attended with great difficulties. An association so
deeply rooted was not so easily disbanded, and, though Jamaica
and the other English colonies in the West Indies were suffered to
be no longer the resting place of villains and rovers, no ordinary
authority could act effectually towards its dispersion. It became,
therefore, absolutely necessary to select a person of their own
caste—a kind of Vidocq—who was thoroughly acquainted with
every detail of the institution, and possessed a perfect knowledge
of the entire ramifications of the piratical system. No man was
better qualified for this service than Henry Morgan, once their
notorious chief, and that those who availed themselves of this
instrument had not miscalculated was sufficiently proved by
subsequent events. Morgan exercised the utmost severity to-

wards his former associates, and was one of the most effectual checks to their future operations.

The destruction of the City of Panama had been so complete that the authorities availed themselves of the opportunity of shifting the settlement from its low and unhealthy position to the little peninsula six miles westward, which communicating only on its western extremity with the main land, and being unapproachable from the sea side by vessels of any size, offered great advantages for defence, and possessed a more salubrious climate, conditions which not only the late invasion dictated, but the health of the colonists demanded. The rebuilding commenced in 1673, two years after Morgan's exploit. The new city was strongly fortified; and, since wood had proved so fatal, all the houses were constructed of stone. Many of the Panamenians were adverse to the shifting of the capital, and still continued residing in the old city—or Panama viejo, as henceforward it was termed—but gradually they followed the common tide; and before many years elapsed the spot was entirely deserted.

The people had good reason to be apprehensive about their security, for the designs of the Buccaneers, though deferred, were not altogether defeated. The maxim of "no peace beyond the line," being duly acknowledged, the war was renewed, and immediately another blow struck against Portobello, which had scarcely revived from its late sack. The attack being successfully accomplished, the rovers shared the spoils to the amount of one hundred and sixty pesos a man. The whole fleet then assembled at Bocas del Toro in the Lagoon of Chiriqui, where intelligence was received that peace had been concluded between the Spaniards and the Indians of Darien; but that the martial Dariens, contrary to the new alliance, had been faithful to Captain Bournano, a

French commander, in his attempt on Chepo, and promised to conduct him to Tocamora, which was said to abound in riches. This information determined their future plans. All agreed to visit the place, and after taking in a supply of tortoises, and refitting the ships, the adventurers' fleet left Bocas del Toro, directing its course towards the east. Another rendezvous and general mustering took place at the Water Key. The whole force was now found to consist of nine sail, amounting to four hundred and forty-eight tons, carrying forty-two guns, and four hundred and seventy-seven men. The largest vessel of one hundred and fifty tons, twenty-five guns and one hundred and seven men, was commanded by Peter Harris, the rest by John Coxon, Richard Sawkins, Bartholomew Sharp, Edmond Cook, Bournano, Alleston, Row and Macket, names most of which attained an unusual degree of notoriety. There was, however, on board of Captain Coxon's ship a person destined for a brighter fame, who amidst the general vice and debauchery around him, faithfully recorded the transactions of this singular association, and transmitted to posterity the most useful account of the discoveries and adventures attending the success of the Buccaneers. This person was William Dampier, a name ever memorable in the Annals of Geographical science, and justly classed among the great naval worthies in which the British Islands have been so prolific. Basil Ringrove and Lionel Wafer, the surgeons, were also men of talent accompanying the expedition. To the former the world is indebted for an account of the proceedings of the Buccaneers, to the latter for his description of Darien. (.1)

The Buccaneers departed from the Water Key towards the

(1) H. W. Smyth Biographical Sketch of Captain Dampier.--History of the Buccaneers. Part IV. Chap. I.

end of 1679, steering for the Samballas group. Not far from Portobello the packet from Carthagena was taken and her letters contained reports of a most singular nature. The merchants of several parts of Old Spain thereby informed their trans-Atlantic correspondents of a certain prophecy current about Spain. There would be that year, it was said, English privateers in the West Indies, who would make such discoveries as to open a door to the South Sea. On arriving at the Samballas Islands, the Indians came to welcome their friends, bringing refreshments and things for barter. The aborigines, however, showed a dislike to the design on Tocamora—probably, because no such place existed— but they were willing to conduct the pirates in secrecy to within a few leagues of Panama. This proposal was approved of by the English, but the French under Bournano and Row, were against a long march over land, and seperated in consequence. The former now reduced to seven sail, were piloted by Andreas, an Indian Chief, to the Golden Island, where tempting information was received of the town of Santa Maria on the Gulf of San Miguel. (2.)

Persuaded by the Indians, they resolved to hazard an attack on Santa Maria, and to proceed thence by sea to Panama (3.) Having taken precautions for guarding the ships, one hundred and thirty-one men were landed on the 5th of April, 1680, all, or most of them, armed with a fusile, a pistol and a hanger, and each man provided besides with four cakes of bread, called dough boys, and toys for the gratification of the natives. The party was accom-

(2) This place must not be confounded with Santamaria la Antigua del Darien, founded by Balboa on the river Darien, which long before this period, had ceased to exist, nor with Santa Maria, the village in the Canton of Nata, Province of Panama. The Santa Maria attacked by the Buccaneers is still in existence: and contained in 1843, according to the census then taken, 204 inhabitants.
(3) History of the Buccaneers, Part IV. Chap I.—W. Smyth, Biographical Sketch of Capt. Dampier.

panied by some of the Dariens, the hereditary foes of the Spaniards; and several of the faithful, active and intelligent Mosquito Indians. On commencing the journey all were marshalled into divisions, with distinguishing flags, under their several commanders, Bartholomew Sharp taking the lead. On the third day of the march an Indian Cacique came in full state to receive the invaders. He wore a garment of white cotton, extending down to his ancles, and a crown curiously constructed of gold, silk and feathers. In his nose hung a large piece of gold shaped like a crescent, and in his ears great rings of the same metal; a bright lance glittering in his hand completed the costume. His wife, three sons and several chiefs accompanied him. The chiefs stood always bare-headed before him, and were clad and armed like himself. His wife wearing a red blanket closely girt around the waist, and another loosely over the head and shoulders, carried a child, and was attended by two daughters, whose faces were painted with red stripes, and whose arms and necks were decorated with beads of various colors. After the Cacique had presented each man with three plantains and some sugar cane to suck, a brisk traffic was opened in which the Indians exhibited an unusual degree of shrewdness. (4.)

A tedious march of nine days brought the Buccaneers to Santa Maria. The place was taken without the loss of a single man on their side. The Spaniards had twenty-six killed and sixteen wounded, and after the surrender many others were deliberately butchered by the Indians. The pirates however were disappointed. Instead of a considerable town which the description of the aborigines led them to anticipate, a miserable village with a small fort, cane huts, and a feeble garrison was found. If the place was

(4) Smyth ibid. History of the Buccaneers. Part IV. Chap. I. II.

bad their fortunes were worse. They arrived only three days too late for three hundred weight of gold which had been shipped for Panama, being the produce of the gold mines of the adjacent country. Moreover the governor, priest, and other persons of rank, from whom large sums might have been extracted, had escaped. After holding Santa Maria for two days, and having deposed Sharp from the chief command and elected Coxon, the Buccaneers on the 17th April 1680, embarked in canoes and boats for the South sea. The greater part of the allies being unwilling to proceed farther left the expedition, though the Cacique and his son, the Cacique Bonete de oro—or king golden cap—as the Spaniards called him, and his kinsman followed. (1.) Ere long two barks were taken, but a third seeing herself chased, made all sail for Panama, and spread the news of the arrival of pirates. The prisoners previously made and others captured at the island of Chepillo, were handed over to the Indians, whose hatred was too deeply rooted to give them any quarter.

On the 23d of April 1680, the *Flotilla* arrived in sight of Panama, but no sooner was it descried than three Spanish ships made towards it, two of which, after a fierce and sanguinary conflict, were carried by boarding; the third saved herself by flight. The Spanish commander with many of his people fell, while of the Buccaneers eighteen men were killed and about thirty wounded, among the latter was Captain Harris, mortally. The valour and skill of Captain Sawkins mainly contributed to the victory, and on Coxon's return to the North sea, he was unanimously chosen commander.

The vessels being overcome all the ships in the port of Perico were made prizes of, and every vessel that entered fell into their

(1) Smyth, ibid. History of the Buccaneers. Part IV., Chap. 3.

hands. Having taken everything within reach, the privateers went to Taboga, Panama being too well prepared for an attack. During their stay at that island they fired the village and received a message from the Governor of Panama, who inquired "why they came to his jurisdiction, and from whom they obtained their commission?" To which Sawkins replied, "their object was to assist the King of Darien, the legitimate lord of the country, and as to the commissions, the company was not yet assembled, but when all were united they would not fail to wait upon him in order to present them." (2.)

Having taken in a supply of provisions at Otoque, their course was directed to the Island of Coyba, on the coast of Veraguas, and thence to Pueblo Nuevo de los Remedios. (3.) There a disaster occurred. Sawkins in leading his men to the assault was slain, and, on his fall, Sharp, the next in command, was so disheartened that he ordered a retreat. The death of the chief proved a serious blow, it being followed by discontent and defections on the part of the men, Sharp being held in great dislike.

Those who remained with the commander now changed their course southward, touching at several islands, taking the coast town of Islay, and burning the city of La Serena on the route. On Christmas-day, they reached Juan Fernandez, where Sharp, who had always been unpopular with the ablest men, and had been chosen by but a small majority, was again formerly deposed, and Capt. Watling elected in his stead. (4.)

---

(2) Smyth, ibid. History of the Buccaneers. Part iv., Chap. 3—8.
(3) There are two places of the name of "Pueblo Nuevo" on the Isthmus, the one situated in the Bay of Panama, is called Pueblo Nuevo de San Carlos, the other standing on the Southern coast of Veraguas, Pueblo Nuevo de los Remedios.
(4) Smyth, ibid. History of the Buccaneers, Part iv., Chap. 9.

On the 12th of January 1681, the Buccaneers were suddenly alarmed by the appearance of three Spanish men-of-war. Neither party being anxious to fight, the ships separated, and the rovers resumed their predatory attacks. At length they made an attempt upon Arica, but were repulsed with loss. Among the slain were Capt. Watling, the boatswain, both quarter-masters, and some of the best hands. Disheartened by this failure, the band of marauders retired to the Isle of Plata. There fresh dissension arose respecting the choice of another chief, and they split into two factions. Before proceeding to an election, it was agreed that the majority together with the new leader should keep the ship, and that the minority should content themselves with the canoes and other small craft. Captain Sharp, who had ingratiated himself with the meaner set, was declared at the head of the poll. Those who voted against him—Dampier among the number—despising a commander so deficient in courage and enterprise, resolved to repass the Isthmus. (1.)

They quitted the ship with the launch and a couple of canoes, their party being composed of forty-four white men, two Mosquito Indians, a Spanish Indian, and five black slaves, and their provisions consisting of about a quarter of a hundred weight of chocolate rubbed up with sugar, and as much flour as they could stow away. All things being prepared, in order to deter the weak or inactive from engaging in so perilous an enterprise, they entered into a mutual compact, that, if any faltered on the journey, he should be killed, as but one man falling into the hands of the enemy must betray the others to certain destruction. (2.)

On approaching the Isthmus, they discovered that the

(1) Smyth, ibid. History of the Buccaneers Part IV., Chap. 10—16.
(2) Smyth's Biographical sketch of Capt. Dampier.

Spaniards were on the look out. Three men-of-war were cruising off the coast, and some hundreds of soldiers posted at different stations along the shore. Though several times in extreme danger, the Buccaneers eluded their foes and safely landed in the bay of San Miguel, where, taking out their effects, they sunk the boats that no traces might be seen. On the 1st of May 1681, they began their march over a country difficult from pathless forests, torrents, rivers and rude mountains, and proceeded to the north-east. On the evening of the second day, when having already become fatigued and dispirited, they fell in with an Indian, who, for the reward of a hatchet, conducted them to a native capable of putting them into the proper route. When, however, they had arrived at his dwelling and explained their wishes, the guide behaved with a sullenness which the Buccaneers could scarcely brook. The moment was critical ; all their lives were in his hands. Every endeavour was used, and recourse had to every means likely to propitiate his good will, but he continued obdurate and replied in angry tones. They began to suspect that he was desirous of handing them over to the Spaniards, when one of the seamen pulling out an azure colored petticoat, threw it over the lady of the house. The woman was so delighted with the gift that she persuaded her husband to give the requisite information and provide a conductor. (3)

Reinforced with a guide, the adventurers resumed their journey. During the greater part of the route, the rain fell in torrents ; the wet season had fairly set in, and, by swelling the streams, frequently compelled the travelers to stop. On one of these occasions, when taking the opportunity of drying their clothes, arms and ammunition, a disaster befel Lionel Wafer, the

(3) Smyth, ibid.

surgeon. He was drying his gunpowder, when one of the party carelessly passed with his pipe and caused an explosion, by which the surgeon's leg was so much burnt, that, after dragging himself forward a few days longer, he was compelled to remain among the Dariens, and four others, who had become exhausted by the march, were reduced to the same necessity.

On the 23d day of the expedition, the Buccaneers procured canoes to carry them down the river Concepcion, and they soon after arrived at La Sound's Key, one of the Samballas Islands. Here the worn-out wanderers embarked on board a French cruiser commanded by Captain Tristian. Their Indian guides returned to their homes, loaded with knives, scissors, hatchets and toys, purchased for the purpose by the Buccaneers out of a privateer. This price of good faith had the happiest effects on the condition of the party left behind with Lionel Wafer. (4.)

The French vessel in which Dampier and his companies embarked, having breamed, was moved over to Springer's Key, another of the Samballas group, where eight more sail, containing upwards of five hundred men, were lying, having assembled for the purpose of making another descent upon Panama. The arrival of the travelers, however, created great commotion. Nothing had been heard of them since the departure of Captain Coxon, a year before. No sooner had Tristian anchored than all the Buccaneer commanders, among the foremost of whom was Coxon himself, repaired on board, and all were overjoyed to see them. After numerous inquiries, the relation of the fatigues and inconveniences undergone, disheartened the listeners from their design, and the assault of other places was taken into consideration. Dampier and his friends were now placed with a Captain

(4) Smyth, ibid.

Archembo because all the other ships were over-manned, but they conceived such a dislike to their foreign shipmaster, that they prevailed on Captain Wright to fit out and arm a prize for them to cruise in. Thus accomodated, the companions sailed from place to place in quest of provisions, being forced to depend upon sea cows, parrots, gulls, boobies, monkeys and wild fruit. (1)

On returning from this cruise to La Sound's Key, guns were fired for the Indians to come on board, in order to obtain tidings of the men left among the Dariens. Those persons having arrived, the signal was immediately answered by their repairing to their old associates. All the natives had vied in attention and kindness to the party, and Lionel Wafer in particular had been treated with distinction by the chief, who, in admiration of his surgical ability, had offered him his daughter in marriage, refusing nothing save the liberty of going away. At length Wafer attempted to obtain permission to depart, under pretext of going in search of English sporting dogs for the copper-colored Nimrod, whose own kennel consisted of dogs that would hardly run by sight or scent. His clothes having been worn out, Wafer had been painted and ornamented by the women, and went about in the Adamite costume. The four seamen, not having been honoured to the same extent, were presently recognised and heartily welcomed by their old shipmates. But Wafer, cringing upon his hams among the Indians, after their fashion, painted as they were and nearly naked, and with his nose piece hanging over his mouth, was willing to try if he would be known in this disguise, and it was the better part of an hour before one, looking more narrowly upon him, cried out: "Why! here's our doctor!" (2.)

. . . .

(1) Smyth, ibid.
(2) Smyth, ibid.

Thus, was completed one of the boldest expeditions ever ventured upon by so small a number of men. It would have been well for the interest of the Isthmenians, and the honor of the Europeans had it been the only one. Unfortunately the road once shown, in spite of the obstacles and dangers it presented, was followed by similar parties. The hatred which the Darien Indians entertained towards the Spaniards, facilitated these undertakings, and the brutal treatment which the unhappy natives had received from their conquerors gave a plausible pretext for disturbing the commerce of a people who had themselves shown so little consideration towards the legitimate children of the soil. But in order to give a still better colour to their atrocities, the rovers always declared that they came to defend the rights of the King or Emperor of Darien, as they emphatically styled him, who—or whose ancestors—enjoyed but a limited authority over a small tribe, as the aborigines, at the time of the conquest, were divided into many independent countries, and had not been brought under the sceptre of one monarch, as the Peruvians or the Aztecs, nor had themselves advanced sufficiently to learn that union is strength.

Though numerous pirates showed themselves from time to time, no serious encroachment on the Spanish territories occurred until the year 1685, when a party of Buccaneers, that had doubled Cape Horn, intercepted a packet-boat, containing intelligence from the Governor of Panama that the Galleon had arrived from Old Spain, and desiring the Plate fleet to hasten its departure from Lima. This intelligence determined the pirates to run for the Pearl Islands, in order to intercept the prize. Their force consisted only of two ships, the *Bachelor's Delight* and the *Cygnet*, the latter commanded by Captain Swan, an Englishman, the former by Captain Davis, a Fleming, two small tenders, a fire ship and a prize. They were moreover aware that the Spaniards were armed and fitted for the avowed purpose of not only defending themselves, but also clearing the Pacific of Buccaneers· Having arrived at the Island of Taboga, the Spaniards made an attempt to set these piratical vessels on fire, but through vigilance and good fortune they escaped by cutting their cables. The following morning while regaining their anchors, they were thrown into consternation at seeing a large fleet of canoes full of men advancing. These proved to be Rovers, who had traversed the Isthmus. There were two hundred French and eighty English, commanded by a Captain Grogniet. The Englishmen joined themselves to the *Bachelor's Delight* and the *Cygnet*, and the Frenchmen were ordered to man the prize. Shortly after, another large party who had travelled over the same road were received on board, so that by a fortuitous train of incidents the force was augmented, in an hour of extreme need, to nine hundred and sixty men, in two ships mounting great guns, and eight smaller vessels with fire-arms. (3.)

For several weeks the freebooting squadron lay nearly opposite Panama, and Davis permitted his men to shoot, fish or pillage among the isles. At length, on the 28th of May, the Spanish fleet hove in sight. According to precise information afterwards obtained from prisoners, it consisted of fourteen sail, besides several peruagos rowing with twelve or fourteen oars a piece. Six sail were large ships; the Admiral, forty-eight guns, three hundred and sixty men; a ship of twenty-four guns, and three hundred men; another of eight guns, two hundred men; two large brûlots, six vessels with small arms, having eight

(3) R. de Lussan—Voyage into the South Sea, 1684, 1689—Smyth Biographical Sketch of Capt. Dampier.

hundred men, besides two or three hundred in the row-boats. Such was the array of that object for which the rovers had so impatiently waited. (4.)

This disparity did not discourage the gallant Davis, who, unacquainted with the fact of the Spanish Admiral having prudently landed the treasure before seeking the fight, resolved to acquire wealth and the dominion of the South Seas, by close combat and boarding. He resolutely bore down upon the advancing foe, and exchanged broadsides till night coming on, he forbore further engagement, as from Swan not acting up to his orders, and Grogniet sheering off without coming into action at all, he was deprived of his most able ships. From a neglect on the part of the Buccaneers, the Spaniards in the night gained the weather-gage, by the simple stratagem of sending a false light to decoy their adversaries to leeward. The loss of this point was fatal to the method of attack proposed by Davis. It enabled the enemy to choose his own distance. Such being the the case, all hopes of conquest vanished with the returning dawn, and the prospective pleasures of riches were superseded by the anxiety of self-preservation. The Spanish ships now became the assailants, steering for them under full sail. There was no alternative for the rovers but to make off, and a running skirmish was maintained till the evening, when having been chased round the Bay of Panama, they anchored at the very place they had quitted in the morning. Thus ended an engagement from which great results had been expected. Instead of making themselves masters of the Spanish fleet and treasure, the pirates were glad to escape. and owed that, too, in a measure, to the want of courage on the part of the Spaniards to pursue their advantage. (1.)

....

(4) Smyth, ibid.
(1) Smyth, ibid.

The dissatisfaction at this discomfiture broke out into reproachful recrimination among the Freebooters. Grogniet excused his conduct by declaring that his men would not let him engage; but this did not satisfy the others; he was consequently cashiered, on their arrival at Coyba, for his cowardly behavior. Some were for taking away the ship which they had so generously given him. At length he was suffered to keep it with his timorous crew; but they were sent away to another place. (2.) Provisions were getting scarce. The Islands of Coyba, though abounding in game and turtles, was uninhabited, and totally unable to maintain so large a body of men. Becoming more distressed, a party on the 30th of June, 1685, made a new attempt on Pueblo Nuevo de los Remedios, which succeeded better than tho first time, but did not supply the deficiency. The assault on other places was taken into consideration. On the 9th of January, 1686, Alanje, the principal town in Chiriqui, was taken and burnt, and on the 18th of November the village of San Lorenzo. A constant cruising was kept up, by means of which many ships were captured, and several treasures intercepted. Though the success by which these exploits were accompanied, tended to make the Buccaneers more daring, and swelled their ranks with fresh recruits, yet it equally prompted the Spaniards to use more precaution and adopt a system of defence which ultimately forced the Rovers to change their field of operations. (3.) The "Treaty of America," concluded in 1670 between England and Spain, though providing for the suppression of the Buccaneers, had proved in this respect merely a piece of waste paper. The war between Great Britain and France in 1688 did more to relieve the Spaniards from this scourge, by disuniting the ancient allies, and

(2) Smth, ibid.
(3) Lussan. Journal of a voyage in the South sea, CHAP. II. III.

the "Treaty of Byswick" in 1697, and four years later the accession of a French Prince to the throne of Spain, gave the final blow to an association which for a century disturbed the commerce of America and checked the industry of its inhabitants.

.   The courage and enterprising spirit which animated this singular association, the hardships and privations its members endured, excite admiration. No science profited more by these than geography, no arts more than commerce and navigation. Seas, coasts and islands, which Spanish jealousy thought fit to close and conceal, were traversed and explored, and a greater number of skilful navigators created, than ever yet proceeded in an equal space of time from the rival States of Europe. Many of the Buccaneers were men of observation, and in perusing their volumes, the most superficial observer must be struck with the familiarity they frequently display with the most minute circumstances. About the Isthmus there was hardly an islet, shoal, or river unknown to them; with the interior their acquaintance was equally extended, and the remarks on the Meteorology, Natural History and Topography do equal credit to the writers. But if the benefits resulting from these exploits receive our approbation, we turn with disgust from the darker side of the picture.   The abominable cruelties the Buccaneers committed, the outrageous proceedings which followed in their track, and the quantity of innocent blood they shed, are crimes which no discovery, however brilliant, can counterbalance, nor any severity of the enemy justify.

While the Isthmus was thus relieved of an association which had long terrified it inhabitants, and disturbed its trade, a company was forming in Scotland for the colonization of Darien. The scheme originated in William Paterson, a clergyman, desirous of visiting foreign parts, and who embarked for the New World under pretext of converting the natives. Visiting various territories, he at last reached the Isthmus of Panama, where he met Captain Dampier and Lionel Wafer. He obtained much information from them, but still more from other old Buccaneers, who, though broken by infirmities and disheartened by misfortunes, recollected with delight, and spoke with rapture of their crossing from sea to sea, carrying valuable booty or driving before them mules richly loaded with plunder. Paterson determined to explore the passage which nature herself seemed to have formed to facilitate commerce, and draw closer the bonds between different nations. In Darien he found a tract of country which the Spaniards had never possessed, and inhabited by a race of Indians who waged continued warfare against them—on the Atlantic side of the Samballas, a group of islands rich in natural productions; the sea abounding with turtle and manaties; at Acla a natural harbor capable of receiving the largest fleet, and sheltered from storms by islands, protected from the enemy by hidden rocks in the entrance; on the opposite shores of the Isthmus harbors of equal excellence, the ridge of hills separating them, though covered with forest, by no means boggy; the soil consisting of rich vegetable mould, producing the finest wild fruits and herbs; and the nature of the territory well adapted for the construction of roads, upon which mules and even carriages could pass in one day from sea to sea. (4)

Paterson knew that ships sailing in a strait line from one point to another and only with one wind, run less risk and require fewer hands, than those passing through many degrees of latitude and along intricate shores, and requiring different winds.

(4) Sir John Dalrymple. Memoirs of Great Britain and Ireland, vol. 2.

He was aware that vessels of eight hundred tons, were found in the South sea managed only by eight or ten sailors, who had little more to do than to make sail on departing, and furl them at the end of the voyage; he was acquainted with the fact that ships from Britain sailing so far south as to meet the trade wind, would be carried to Darien, and that the same wind would take vessels from the Bay of Panama to the East Indies and *vice versa*; that ships steering from the East Indies to the Bay of Panama, after having reached the 40th degree of northern latitude, would fall in with the westerly wind, blowing in those regions with the regularity of the trades, and which would carry them to the Mexican coast; and that the land and sea breezes would bring them to the Bay of Panama.   Hence he concluded that vessels departing from Britain, except on the voyage to the South, in the latitude of the trade winds, and those from the East Indies, except on the voyage to the North in the regions of the westerly winds, and ships from the other side of the Isthmus to the East would not encounter uncertain winds.

Gold was found in different places, but this discovery he regarded of less value.   His attention was directed to objects of greater importance—the shortening of distances, the closer communication of nations, the preservation of the lives of seamen and the saving of time and freightage.   Paterson in fact conceived the idea of planting on this neglected spot a great and powerful colony, which unlike most settlements of a similar kind, should not be established by accident, or unprotected by their native country, but be founded on a system well conceived, and under the protection of those governments to whom the project was to be offered. (1.)

(1) Dalrymple, ibid.

The first power to whom Paterson intended to propose the scheme was England. That country he thought had the most interest in it, not only from the advantages he would derive from the shortening of the voyages to the East Indies, but from the effect it would produce between her dominions. Paterson however had only a few friends, and no interest in London, and to excite public attention and gain the approbation of rich and influential men, he assisted the latter in modelling a plan for the Bank of England, which was then—in the year 1694 - in contemplation. But he found to his mortification what many others had experienced. The persons whom he so generously obliged, and who, he expected, would further his object, made use of his ideas, took the honor of them, were polite to him for some time, and neglected him afterwards. He now communicated his project to only a few, and these few discouraged him. He next offered his scheme to the Dutch, the Hamburgers, and the Elector of Brandenburg. The Dutch and Hamburg merchants, who had the most interest in the object of his visit, listened to him with indifference, the Elector of Brandenburg, who was little interested in the scheme, received him with distinction, but court arts and intrigues to which the honest clergyman was a stranger, soon deprived him of the favor of this prince. (2.)

Paterson seeing that neither in Germany nor in Holland he could attain his object, returned to London, where he made the acquaintance of Andrew Fletcher of Saltown, who was enthusiastic about all things conducive to public prosperity. He accompanied Paterson to Scotland and introduced him to the Marquis of Tweedale, then Minister for the Scot Kingdom. Fletcher persuaded that nobleman that it would be for the good of the people,

----

(2) Dalrymple, ibid.

and the honor of his administration to accept Paterson's proposal. Lord Stair and Mr. Johnson, the two Secretaries of State, entered into Paterson's plans, and Sir James Stuart, the Lord Advocate, a relation of Stair, went the same road. In June 1695, these men succeeded in obtaining the Act of Parliament, and afterwards a Charter from the crown, to establish commercial companies in Africa and America, with the authority to plant colonies and erect forts, by the consent of the aborigines, at places not yet in possession of European nations.

Paterson who now began to feel solid ground under his feet and perceived that he was assisted by the power and talents of his native country, and possessed the confirmation of an Act of Parliament and Royal Charter, made the parties acquainted with his project and collected subscriptions for the formation of a company. The rage of the Scots to sign the solemn league and covenant never exceeded the rapidity with which they incorporated their names in the Darien Company. Nobility, gentry, merchants, people, the Royal Burghs without exception, and most of the other public bodies subscribed in a short space of time more than £400,000, although at that period no more than £800,000 cash were said to exist in the whole Kingdom. Paterson's project which was received by foreigners with fear and distrust when disclosed in secret, filled them with hope when coming on the wings of fame. The English forthwith subscribed £300,000, and the Dutch and Hamburgers £200,000. (3.)

Commercial jealousy which had so long been silent in England, began now to display itself with the utmost violence. On the 13th December, 1695, both Houses of Parlament agreed,

(3) Dalrymple, ibid.

without previous enquiry or consideration, to protest, in an address to the King, against the establishment of the Darien Company, as an undertaking injurious to the interest of the East India Company. The English House of Commons soon after, on the 26th of January, 1696, accused some of its own countrymen and several Scots, among them a Peer, Lord Belhaven, of being guilty of high crime and misdemeanor by assisting in establishing the Darien Company. Among six hundred legislators not one had the prudence of proposing or rather the boldness to propose, a committee to inquire into the principles and importance of the institution. But at that period a lamentable degree of corruption prevailed in the English Parliament. Many of the members did not shrink from accepting sums from the East India Company, for facilitating bills relating to that body; and it could hardly be expected that under such circumstances, where personal interest was mingled with national prejudice, members should be found ready to expose the injustice of the proceedings. King William's answer to the address was: "I have had bad councillors in Scotland." Soon after he changed his Scottish ministers, and to crown the success of the opposition, sent a memorandum to the Senate of Hamburg, warning it against any connection with the Company. The Senate transmitted the memorandum to the Chamber of Commerce, who returned it with the following reply: "We are surprised.to see the King of Britain attempting to hinder us, a free people, from opening communication with whom we please, and we are astonished to perceive that His Majesty intends to prevent us from holding connection with his own subjects in Scotland, on whom he has lately conferred by act of Parliament, such extensive privi-

leges." But the mercantile mind was then as now, rather
fickle; and soon after Hamburg, Holland and London withdrew
their subscriptions. (4.)

The Scots far from being disheartened by the violence of
the opposition, became only more eager to carry out their plans
of colonization, and they considered it merely as a proof of the
envy of the English and jealousy of the advantages Scotland
was to derive from her settlement. The Darien Company
ordered six ships to be built in Holland, and engaged twelve
hundred colonists. Among them were the sons of noble ancient
families, and sixty officers, who had retired at the commencement of the peace. None but select people accompanied them,
principally those who had been brought up on their own or
their relations' estates, of whose courage they were certain and
of whose attachment there was no doubt. On the 5th August,
1698, the Scottish Parliament appealed to the King, imploring
him to assist the Company. The Lord President, Sir Hugh
Dalrymple, brother of Lord Stair and head of the bench, and
the Lord Advocate, Sir James Stuart, head of the bar, jointly
addressed petitions to His Majesty, in which they defended the
rights of the Company, upon the principles of Constitutional
and Public law. But all was in vain. The neighboring States
saw with surprise and admiration, the poorest Kingdom of
Europe dispatching a colony such as never before had left the
European shores. (1.)

In the beginning of September, 1699, the preparations for
the Colony had been completed. On the starting day all Edin-
burgh poured down Leith to see the emigrants depart. So
eager were the Scots to embark that many seamen, whose

(4) J. Wade, British History, chronologically arranged. Third edition, p. 281.
(1) Dalrymple, ibid.

services had been rejected on account of the number of applications, were concealed on board the ships, and when ordered on shore, they clung to the masts and ropes, imploring the authorities for merely a passage. One thousand five hundred persons embarked in five stout ships, and arrived in Darien on the 4th November, after a voyage of two months, without losing more than fifteen of their number. Their first object was to buy land from the natives, send messengers of peace to the Spanish Governors, and settle at Acla, calling the place, after the patron Saint of Scotland, New St. Andrew, and the country adjacent New Caledonia. (2.)

Acla is memorable in more than one respect. A few years previous to the Spanish discovery of this coast two brothers reigned over the district, each striving for supreme power, and looking with an envious eye upon his rival. The mutual discontent broke out at last in open violence. Both took up arms, to let force determine what discussion was unable to settle. The warriors approached each other at Acla, and so enraged were the chiefs, and so eager their followers, that great masses perished before the parties dispersed. At the arrival of the Spaniards, the bones of the slain were still bleaching in the sun, regarded with awe by the native, with horror by the Castilian. Pedrarias Davila, delighted with the richness of the adjacent country, erected then in 1515, a fortress in which a few years later he sacrificed the lives of the gallant Balboa and his enterprising companions. The uncultivated Indian named the place Acla—or men's bones—arena of envy would have been a more appropriate appellation; for the same passion which prompted the brother to lift up the hand against his brother, inspired

(2) Dalrymple, ibid. Wade, ibid, page 287.

Davila to execute the discoverer of the South Sea, and also was to prove the ruin of the honest Scot. (3.)

The Colonists set actively to work improving the harbor of Acla—or as it is now termed Puerto de Escoces. A canal was cut and a fort erected on which fifty guns were planted. On one side of the port rose a hill about a mile high, where a watch-house was built which gave them an extensive survey, and guarded against surprise. The Highlanders were often observed enjoying the cool air of this hill, and talking of home and friends—friends whose expectations were as high as their mountains. The first public act of the colony was a proclamation declaring commercial and religious liberty. This great idea which, even at the present day, few nations are fully able to appreciate, originated in the enlightened mind of Paterson. (4) .

Meanwhile the East India Company, aided by the English, pursuaded the King to ruin the Colony. Orders were dispatched to the Governors of the Indian and American possessions to issue proclamations, prohibiting all assistance to the emigrants or connection with them. The Scots, who expected a far different treatment, had not taken sufficient provisions, and being suddenly cut off, they fell sick from want of food. The Indians were more generous to them, and by hunting and fishing gave that aid which Europeans so disgracefully refused. But they were unable to support so large a body of men. Eight months passed and no succour arrived; in vain the sufferers looked over the broad ocean, no friendly bark appeared, despair seized the boldest heart, and nearly all died or left the fatal spot. (1.)

(3) Herrera, Decad II, Libro II, Cap. I. and Decad II, Libro III, Cap. V. Herrera Decad IV, Libro I, Cap. X.
(4) Dalrymple, ibid.
(1) Dalrymple, ibid.

During the two years the establishment of the Colony had been going on, Spain had raised no complaints against Scotland. The Darien Council asserts even in its documents, that, previous to the departure of the settlers, the rights of the Company had been discussed before the King of Spain, and in presence of the Scotch Ambassador. But now the Spanish Ambassador in London transmitted a note in which he complained of the settlement in Darien, as an encroachment on the rights of his master. The Scotch, unacquainted with the misfortune of the Colony, but vexed about this note, sent a reinforcement of one thousand three hundred men to assist an establishment which already had ceased to exist. This party had been prepared more hastily, and was unfortunate in the voyage. One of the ships was wrecked, many of the emigrants died on board, and the rest arrived at Darien at different times, mostly sick, and disheartened on hearing the misfortunes of their predecessors. To add to the calamity of the first Colony, the second had its peculiar disasters. The assembly of the Scotch Kirk had sent four clergymen with orders to elect ecclesiastical government functionaries, and establish Divine Service. On arriving at Darien the four delegates found the officers and gentlemen employed building houses with their own hands, as no assistance could be obtained from others; yet they complained that no instant orders were given to erect houses for them. Not having taken the precaution to bring letters from the Directors to the Darien Council, they were not received with the attention they expected by the higher class of colonists. They therefore directed themselves to the lower settlers, and gave rise to many dissentions. They exhausted the patience of the people by long service, lasting four or five hours. In addition to the usual

observance of the Sabbath, Wednesday was selected for a day
of devotion ; and so much was the regular service augmented
that it frequently lasted twelve hours without interruption, the
congregation assembling in a garrison room. All this occurred
in an unhealthy season of a tropical climate, and could not have
had other but prejudical effects on the health of the colonists.
Nor did these fanatics stop here. They wrote and promulgated
an address to the Council, in which they demanded an additional
day to be devoted to fasting and humiliation. The reason
assigned was the sins of the colonists, in enumerating which
they did not fail to heap abuse upon the authorities. They
discouraged the people by constantly representing hell as the
end of all the lives of most men, and carrying the doctrine of
predestination to an extreme point, they prevented all exertion.
Forced at last to leave the settlement, they tried to exculpate
themselves by writing libels to the General Assembly against
the character and advantages of the Colony. (2.)

At the time these events happened in Darien, the parties in
Britain were actively contending, and on the 12th February,
1700, the English House of Lords addressed the King against
the re-establishment of the Scotch Colony. The delicate position of William III. can be imagined. An elected monarch and
sovereign over a people in whom national prejudices and party
feelings were yet at their height, he was worse than powerless.
In pleasing the one he offended the other, in countenancing the
Scots he enraged the English. In the question before him he
steered a course best suited to his sagacity ; he again proposed a
Union between England and Scotland, but this proposal was
once more rejected.

(2) Dalrymple, ibid.

At the same time the Commons resolved that a book, entitled " An Enquiry into the Causes of the Miscarriages of the Scotch Colony at Darien," was a false, scandalous, and traitorous libel, and ordered it to be burnt by the hangman, and issued a proclamation for apprehending the author. The Scots were equally eager. They petitioned the King (Feb. 25, 1700,) to call a parliament in that Kingdom, in order to re-establish the affairs of their American and East India Company, which they apprehended labored under very great hardships both at home and abroad. The King promised that their Parliament should meet. At a sitting on the 21st of May, 1700, a vote was proposed: "That the Colony of Darien was a loyal and rightful settlement, and that the Parliament would maintain and support it." But the High Commissioner adjourned them from time to time, to prevent the question being put, of which the Scotch complained in a national address to King William. (3.)

After the second party of colonists had been settled three months, they were joined by Captain Campbell and a body of men from his estates whom he had commanded in Flanders, and brought in his own ship to Darien. On their arrival at New St. Andrew, all was in consternation, intelligence having been received that a Spanish force of sixteen hundred men had arrived from the coast of the South sea and was encamped at Ibuganti, awaiting only the co-operation of a naval squadron to attack the settlement. The Scots determined to commence hostilities before the junction took place. The supreme command having been conferred on Captain Campbell, for his reputation as a soldier, they marched to Inbuganti. The enterprise proved successful. During the night the enemy was surprised and dispersed

(3) J. Wade, ibid, pape 288 and 289.

with slaughter. On the fifth day, Captain Campbell returned
to New St. Andrew. The Spanish fleet had arrived, the troops
had been landed, and nearly all hopes of succour cut off. He
threw himself in the fort, and in spite of all disadvantages, stood
a close siege for six weeks, until the greater part of the officers
were killed. The enemy in advancing had cut off the water, all
their shot was expended, and for the balls recourse was obliged
to be had to the pewter vessels of the garrison. Resistance
being hopeless, the colonists accepted an honorable capitulation.
Not only did they obtain the honors of war, but the property of
the Company was respected, and, as if the Scotch had been the
victors, hostages were sent for the faithful execution of the
conditions. Campbell alone refused to accept the capitulation.
The Spaniards, he said, could never forgive him the injury he
had inflicted. The brave often escape that death which they
seem to challenge. Campbell succeeded in effecting his escape
on board his ship, and safely reached Scotland. The Company
presented him with a gold medal with a flattering inscription, and
Lord Lyon, King at Arms, gave him an Indian and a Highlander
as supporters of his coat of arms. (4.)

A severer fate awaited those whom Campbell had left at
Darien. Their health was so much weakened that they were
unable to weigh the anchor of the *Rising Sun*, one of their ships
with sixty guns; but the Spaniards generously assisted them.
When the vessel left the harbor it stranded, but even here the
enemy showed forbearance, though to make the ruin complete,
they need have done nothing more than look on. The ships,
leaky and badly manned, were repeatedly obliged to seek shelter
in Spanish and English ports. The Spaniards showed them

(4) Dalrmyple, ibid.

kindness, the English Governors the contrary, and at one place a ship was detained and seized. Of all the vessels only that of Captain Campbell and a small one were saved. The *Rising Sun* was stranded on the bar of Charlestown; and of this powerful Colony no more than thirty souls who had been saved from war, ship-wreck, famine, and disease, reached their native country. (1)

Paterson, who had firmly borne the misfortune, sunk under its reaction. On the homeward voyage he became lunatic. He recovered in his native country, and with a spirit still active and unbroken, he presented a new plan, founded on the idea of King William, that England and Scotland should have jointly possession of the settlement. He lived afterwards many years in Scotland, pitied, respected, but neglected. After the union of the kingdoms (1707) he claimed compensation for his losses, out of the money paid by England, as amends to the Darien Company. However, he received nothing. Poor Paterson! How different might have been his fate if the project had succeeded! How different the aspect of Spanish America! By spreading liberal, religious, political and commercial ideas, the influence of the Colony would, probably, have shaken to the very foundation the system of blind superstition practised in that country, given the death blow to Spanish despotism, paved the way for the abolition of commercial monopolies, and conducted the inhabitants at an earlier period to that state of civil and religious liberty, which, during the present century they have made such efforts to obtain.

----

(1) Dalrymple, ibid.

Aug. Clement.   L. S. Bethancourt.

ASPINWALL HOTEL,

CORNER MAIN & JIRALDOT STS.

PANAMA.

THIS WELL-KNOWN AND FAVORITE HOTEL which has just undergone the most complete renovation in all its departments, is the largest, most convenient, and best on the Isthmus. It contains very fine, airy, and well furnished Bedrooms, a splendid Reception Room, large and pleasant Dining Halls, Bath-rooms, Bar-room, and all the requirements of a first-class Hotel. The Culinary Department is under the superintendence of the senior Proprietor,

Monsieur CLEMENT,

assisted by the best of French cooks, and the table is bountifully supplied with all the luxuries procurable in this market as well as from abroad.

Persons visiting the HOTEL will always meet with kind and obliging Proprietors and polite servants.

N.B.—The best of all kinds of Wines and Cigars of our own importation.

CLEMENT & BETHANCOURT.

THE PACIFIC MAIL STEAMSHIP COMPANY'S

THROUGH LINE OF STEAMERS BETWEEN NEW YORK, SAN FRANCISCO, JAPAN AND CHINA, VIA THE ISTHMUS.

THIS COMPANY now performs a THRICE MONTHLY Service between NEW YORK and SAN FRANCISCO, with ELEGANT NEW STEAMERS, built expressly for the trade, and fitted up with an especial view to the comfort of Passengers.

DATES OF DEPARTURE FROM NEW YORK—1st, 11th and 21st, (or on Saturday, when these dates fall on Sunday.)

DATES OF ARRIVAL AT ASPINWALL (COLON)—9th, 19th & 29th.

DATES OF DEPARTURE FROM ASPINWALL (COLON) FOR NEW YORK—1st, 12th or 13th, and 23rd.

DATES OF DEPARTURE FROM PANAMA FOR SAN FRANCISCO—9th, 19th and 29th—Steamer of the 9th touches at Manzanillo, and all at Acapulco.

DATES OF DEPARTURE FROM SAN FRANCISCO—10th, 19th and 30th—(or on Saturday, when these dates fall on Sunday.)

ARRIVAL AT PANAMA—1st, 12th or 13th, and 22nd or 23rd.

THE SECOND STEAMER FOR JAPAN & CHINA

Will leave San Francisco, April 3rd, 1867, (the Steamer leaving Panama on or about 19th March, connecting with her) and due notice of subsequent voyages will be given.

Cargo taken under Through Bills of Lading to New York or San Francisco, upon application to the Agents of the Pacific Steam Navigation Company on the South-west Coast, and to those of the Panama Railroad Company on the Central American Coast.

Through Bills of Lading will also be issued for San Francisco by the Agent of the Compagnie Generale Transatlantique at St. Nazaire, by the Agent of the Royal West India Mail Company at Southampton, and by the Agent of the West India and Pacific Steamship Company at Liverpool.

Through Passage Tickets for this line issued by the Agents of the Pacific Steam Navigation Company at the ports on the South-west Coast.

THROUGH TICKETS TO LIVERPOOL issued by this line, connecting at NEW YORK with the Steamers of the

CUNARD ROYAL MAIL LINE; INMAN LINE; NATIONAL STEAM NAVIGATION CO.;

ALSO TO HAVRE BY THE STEAMERS OF THE

GENERAL TRANSATLANTIC STEAMSHIP COMPANY.

For further information, apply to

D. M. CORWINE, Agent, Panama.

G. B. GIBBONS, Agent, Aspinwall.

COMPAGNIE GENERALE
TRANSATLANTIQUE.

---◆---

MONTHLY SERVICE.

---◆---

WITHOUT TRANSHIPMENT BETWEEN THE PORTS OF
ASPINWALL (COLON) AND ST. NAZAIRE, FRANCE.
TOUCHING AT SANTA MARTHA, U.S.C.,
· AND
PORT ROYAL, MARTINIQUE.

---◆·◆---

THE STEAMERS leave St. Nazaire on the 8th of each month, arrive at Aspinwall on the 28th or 29th of each month, and leave for St. Nazaire on the 1st or 2nd connecting with the steamer from the South which arrives at Panama on the 28th, with the steamer from Central America which arrives on the 30th, and with the steamer from California which arrives on the 1st.

Arrival at St. Nazaire on the 23d of each month, after 21 days'
· PASSAGE.

Passengers bound for the Continent of Europe should take this route, as it not only offers the best and cheapest accommodations, but owing to the ramifications of the French Railroads, on disembarking at Saint Nazaire every facility is afforded for continuing their journey to their different destinations.

The Company will grant to Shippers of Produce from the Pacific Coast and the Isthmus, Policies of Insurance on advantageous terms.

The Company will also at a later date, by arrangements with the railroads of the Continent, undertake the forwarding of Cargo to all commercial towns of Europe, affording all possible facilities to shippers who have no correspondents at St. Nazaire.

The GENERAL TRANSATLANTIC COMPANY desirous of developing as much as possible the traffic between America and France, has authorized its Agents in Aspinwall and Panama to arrange rates of freight from Panama and Aspinwall to St. Nazaire on produce of the Isthmus, and that which is received at both ports; and issue Through Bills of Lading to Havre, Bordeaux, Holland, Bremen and Hamburg.

Arrangements have also been made for booking passengers through, and giving Through Bills of Lading for Freight between St. Nazaire and the Pacific ports of Central and South America, Mexico and California.

For Freight or Passage, Apply to
J. B. F. ARRIVET, Agent in Colon,
HOURQUET, POYLO & CO.,
CORRESPONDENTS—PANAMA,
and all the Agents of Steamship Lines in the North and South Pacific.

STEAM COMMUNICATION WITH AUSTRALASIA.

PANAMA, NEW ZEALAND AND AUSTRALIAN ROYAL MAIL COMPANY (LIMITED.)

THE STEAMERS of the above Company arrive at Panama from the Australasian Colonies on the 4th or 5th of each month, and sail from Panama to Wellington, New Zealand, forwarding passengers and merchandise from thence to Sydney, Melbourne, and all the principal ports in New Zealand, including Auckland, Napier, Nelson, Lyttleton, Dunedin, &c., &c. Special Steamers are appointed to sail to meet the continued influx of emigrants to the newly discovered gold regions of Hokitika.

An experienced and qualified Surgeon accompanies each Steamer, and in the construction and conduct of the Company's ships especial care has been observed to secure the comfort of passengers.

The unvarying punctuality of the Steamers of the Company in forming their several connections on the ten first successive voyages, guarantees safety and rapidity of transit.

The Company's Steamers arriving from the Colonies on the 4tb or 5th, connect with the following steamers from the Isthmus:

For South Pacific sailing on the 10th of each month.
" California " " 9th " month.
" Central America " " 10th " month.
" New York " " 12th or 13th of each month.
" Southampton " " 6th or 7th of each month.
" Havana " " 5th or 6th of each month.

The following arrivals at the Isthmus of Panama connect with the Steamers for the Colonies on the 24th of each month:

From South Pacific arriving on the 19th of each month.
" California " " 22d or 23d of each month.
" Central America " " 15th of each month.
" New York " " 19th month.
" Southampton " " 22d " month.
" Havana " " " month.

Passengers conveyed to the Colonies at fares varying from $280 to $300 first Class, according to distance and accommodation. Second Class fares $150 to $175.
1st Class Passengers allowed 336lbs Baggage.
2nd Class Passengers allowed 168lbs Baggage.
Children and Servants conveyed at proportionate rates.
Return Tickets issued at a reduction of 25 per cent.
Freight from $50 to $70 per ton, according to class and distance of destination.
Fu ther information on application to

W. LANE BOOKER, Agent, San Francisco.
CHARLES W. WEST, Agt. New York.
WILLIAM G. SEALY, Agt. Panama.

And to all the Agencies of the Pacific Steam Navigation Co. in the South Pacific; also to the Agencies of the Pacific Mail Steamship Company at New York, San Francisco and Panama.
Panama, April 8, 1867.

ROYAL MAIL STEAM PACKET CO.

UNDER CONTRACT WITH HER MAJESTY'S GOVERNMENT,

FOR THE CONVEYANCE OF THE MAILS FOR THE

West Indies, Mexico, Central America, North and South Pacific, New Zealand and

AUSTRALIAN COLONIES.

THE following arrangement, for the Mail Service, has been recently sanctioned by Her Britannic Majesty's Government:—

1.—The Steamers from Southampton will proceed to Peter Island and Jamaica—returning by the same course to Southampton

2.—The windward Steamers will communicate with the outward and homeward Steamers at Peter Isl nd.

3.—The Steamers for Porto Rico, Cuba and Mexico, will communicate with the outward and homeward Steamers at Peter Island.

4.—The direct Steamers to and from Colon, will communicate monthly with the outward and homeward Steamers at Peter Island; the other Steamers to and from Colon communicating with the outward and homeward Steamers at Jamaica as heretofore.

5.—There will only be a monthly communication with Jacmel—namely, hence on the middle of each month, the return Steamer bringing the Mail from Jacmel at the end of each month.

The Company's steamers leave Southampton on the 2d and 17th of each month, and Colon (Aspinwall) on the 6th and 23d of each month.

On their arrival at Peter Island other steamers belonging to the Company are ready to convey Mails, Passengers, &c., to the following named places : St. Kitts, Antigua, Guadeloupe, Dominica, Martinique, St. Lucia, Barbadoes, Demerara, St. Vincent, Grenada, Trinidad, Tobago, St. Thomas, Jamaica, Porto Rico, Havana, Vera Cruz and Tampico.

The Company's steamers to and from Colon (Aspinwall) connect on the Isthmus of Panama with the Australian, South Pacific, California, Japan, China and Central American steamers.

A monthly service for the conveyance of Mails, Passengers, &c., is also established by the Company's Steamers between Colon, Carthagena and Santa Martha, and between these places and Grey Town, connecting at Colon with the steamers to Southampton and intermediate and branch ports.

The Steamers leaving Aspinwall on the 6th connect with the Steamers for Havana, New Orleans, Vera Cruz and Tampico.

Further information may be obtained at the Company's Office, 55, Moorgate street, London, or from C. A. Henderson, Esq., H. B. M.'s Consul, Panama; D. R. Martin, Esq., Agent, Colon, and at the Agencies of connecting Companies.

STEAMSHIP COMBINATIONS ON THE ISTHMUS.

ROYAL WEST INDIA MAIL STEAMERS.

The Steamers of this line leave Southampton on the 2d and 17th of each month, arriving at Aspinwall on the 7th or 8th and 22d, and connect with the Steamers of the Pacific Steam Navigation Company, sailing from Panama for Guayaquil, Callao and Valparaiso on the 9th or 10th and 25th, and with the Steamers of the Panama Railroad Company sailing for Costa Rica, Nicaragua, Salvador and Guatemala on the 10th and 25th. The Steamer arriving at Aspinwall on the 7th or 8th, connects with the steamer of the Pacific Mail Steamship Company which sails from Panama on the 9th for San Francisco, touching at Acapulco and Manzanillo, Mexico, and the steamer arriving on the 22d connects with the New Zealand and Australian Steamer sailing on the 24th.

A steamer leaves Aspinwall for Greytown, Nicaragua on the 9th, returning on the 17th, and one for Carthagena and Santa Martha on the 24th returning on the 3rd.

These steamers leave Aspinwall for Southampton via Jamaica and Peter Island on the 5th or 6th and 23rd. The first steamer in each month only connects with the Steamer for Havana, which connects with the Steamer thence to New Orleans.

PACIFIC STEAM NAVIGATION COMPANY.

The Steamers of this line leave Valparaiso on the 3rd, 10th and 17th, and Callao on the 14th, 22d and 28th, arriving at Panama on the morning of the 3rd or 4th, 20th, and 29th, and connect with the Royal West India Mail Company's Steamers sailing from Aspinwall for Southampton via St. Thomas on the 5th or 6th and 23rd, and with the Steamer of the Compagnie Generale Transatlantique sailing from Aspinwall for St. Nazaire on the 31st or 1st. The steamer arriving at Panama on the 3rd or 4th connects with the Steamer leaving St. Thomas for Havana and Vera Cruz on the 14th, and the Steamers arriving at Panama on the 20th and 29th, connect with the steamers leaving Aspinwall for New York; they will also connect with the steamers leaving Aspinwall for Liverpool on the 10th and 25th, and with the Steamer leaving Panama on the 29th for San Francisco touching at Acapulco.

A Steamer leaves Panama for Buenaventura, Guayaquil, Callao and intermediate ports on the 12th of each month.

These Steamers leave Panama for the South Coast on the 1st, 9th or 10th and 25th.

PACIFIC MAIL STEAMSHIP COMPANY.

The Steamers of this line on the Pacific leave San Francisco on the 10th, 19th (18th when the month has only 30 days) and 30th, (or on the previous Saturday when these days fall on Sunday,) and arrive at Panama on the 1st, 12th or 13th and 22d or 23rd of each month, connecting with the steamers of the same Company leaving Aspinwall for New York on the 1st, 12th or 13th and 23rd. These steamers will connect with the Steamers leaving here for the South Pacific on the 1st, 13th and 25th, with the W. I. & P. S. S. Co's steamers which sail from Aspinwall for Liverpool on the 10th and 25th. The Steamer arriving on the 23d connects with the Royal West India Mail Company's steamer sailing from Aspinwall for Southampton on the same day, and the Steamer arriving on the 1st connects with the French Steamer for St. Nazaire.

The Atlantic Steamers of this line will leave New York on the 1st, 11th and 21st (or on the previous Saturday when these days fall on Sunday,) and arrive at Aspinwall on the 9th, 19th and 29th, connecting with the steamers of the same Company leaving Panama for San Francisco, touching at Acapulco, Mexico, on the 9th, 19th and 29th; the steamer of the 9th touches at Manzanillo also. The steamers arriving at Aspinwall on the 9th and 29th will connect with the Steamers for the South Pacific, which leave Panama on the 1st and 10th. The steamer arriving on the 9th will also connect with the steamer for Central America which sails from Panama on the 10th. The steamer arriving on the 19th connect with the New Zealand and Australian steamer leaving Panama on the 24th.

PANAMA RAILROAD COMPANY'S CENTRAL AMERICAN STEAMERS.

The Steamers of this line sail from San José de Guatemala on the 20th and 5th, touching at ports in Salvador, Nicaragua and Costa Rica, and arrive at Panama on the 16th and 30th, connecting with the West India and Pacific Steamship Company's steamers leaving Aspinwall for Liverpool about the same time. The steamer arriving at Panama on the 30th connects with the steamer for New York, which leaves Aspinwall on the 1st, with the steamer of the Compagnie Generale Transatlantique leaving Aspinwall on the 31st or 1st, and with the South Pacific Steamer sailing from Panama on the 1st.

Passengers from Central America for Europe via the Royal West India Mail Company's steamers will be detained on the Isthmus six days.

These steamers sail from Panama on the 10th and 25th.

WEST INDIA AND PACIFIC STEAMSHIP COMPANY, LIMITED.

The steamers of this line sail from Aspinwall via Jamaica for Liverpool on the 10th and 25th, arriving at Liverpool on the 12th and 27th, and convey freight and passengers to England brought by the steamers from the South Pacific, Central America, California and Australia.

COMPAGNIE GENERALE TRANSATLANTIQUE.

The steamers of this line leave St. Nazaire, France, on the 8th of each month, arriving at Aspinwall on the 28th or 29th, and connect with the South Pacific steamer sailing on the 1st, and the North Pacific steamers, [for San Francisco, Acapulco, &c.] sailing on the 31st or 1st of each month, touching at Santa Martha and Martinique, and take passengers and merchandize from the South Pacific steamer arriving at Panama on the 29th; the Panama Railroad Company's Central American steamer arriving at Panama on the 30th, and the North Pacific [San Francisco and Acapulco] steamer arriving on the 31st.

THE PANAMA, NEW ZEALAND AND AUSTRALIAN MAIL COMPANY'S STEAMERS.

The Panama, New Zealand and Australia Company's steamers arrive at Panama on the 4th or 5th of each month, connecting with the Royal West India Mail Company's steamers sailing for Southampton on the 5th or 6th.

These steamers sail hence for Wellington on the 24th, taking passengers arriving from the South Pacific on the 20th, from New York on the 19th, from California on the 23d, and from England on the 22d.

THE SPANISH MAIL PACKET COMPANY IN THE ANTILLES AND GULF OF MEXICO.

The steamer Moctezuma leaves Havana on the 22d of each month, and arrives at Aspinwall on the 4th, touching at Nuevitas, Gibara, Santiago de Cuba, Jamaica, Santa Martha and Carthagena. Leaves Aspinwall on the 5th or 6th and arrives at Havana on the 17th, touching at Jamaica, Santiago de Cuba, Baracoa, Gibara and Nuevitas.

PACIFIC NAVAL STORE.

WILLIAM DE ROUX,

Commission Merchant and Forwarding Agent.

PURVEYOR AND CONTRACTOR

TO THE

ENGLISH, FRENCH & SPANISH NAVIES,

IMPORTER OF ENGLISH, FRENCH & AMERICAN DRY GOODS, PROVISIONS, WINES AND LIQUORS.

AGENT FOR THE IMPERIAL FIRE INSURANCE COMPANY OF LONDON.

SOLE AGENT FOR MEDLEY & SON'S LIVERPOOL SOAP,

AND FOR

ALLSOP'S PALE ALE AND STOUT, BOTTLED BY F. FRIEND & CO.

ADVANCES MADE ON CONSIGNMENTS OF PRODUCE.

PACIFIC NAVAL STORE.

WILLIAM DE ROUX,

BANKER,

Corresponding Agent of the Union Bank of London, London Joint Stock Bank, City Bank of London and Asiatic Banking Corporation.

HENRY EHRMANN,
HAVANA CIGAR DEPOT,
AND
FANCY STORE,
PANAMA, U.S.C.,
Has always on hand, at moderate prices, a fine assortment of
BEST HAVANA CIGARS,
SMOKING AND CHEWING TOBACCO,
imported direct.
PANAMA HATS IN GREAT VARIETY,
Chinese and Japanese Ware of every description ; Silver Card Cases, Fans, &c.,
PAMAMA JEWELRY, PEARLS, &c.
GENTLEMEN'S TOILET GOODS
of all kinds, and a large assortment of articles too numerous to mention.
Passengers will find this Store just the place to visit to buy nic-nacks & curiosities.

THE GRAND HOTEL,
CATHEDRAL SQUARE,
PANAMA, U. S. C.

THIS MAGNIFICENT ESTABLISHMENT which was opened on the 1st of March, is acknowledged to be unequalled in elegance and comfort in South America. It has been constructed under the direct superintendence of the Proprietor, in the most approved style, and is fitted up with the best French furniture.

The location is the finest in Panama, commanding an extensive view of the Bay, and fronting on the Square. The rooms are large, well ventilated, and admirably adapted for a tropical climate; and each landing is plentifully supplied with Baths, Water Closets, &c.

The BAR, BILLIARD SALOONS, DINING HALLS and RECEPTION ROOMS are elegantly fitted up; the Table is supplied with every luxury, and the Bar with the best WINES and LIQUORS, imported direct from France by the Proprietor.

ICE CREAMS EVERY EVENING.
PRIVATE SALOON FOR LADIES.
GEORGE LOEW,
Proprietor.

www.ingramcontent.com/pod-product-compliance
Lightning Source LLC
Chambersburg PA
CBHW020245090426
42735CB00010B/1846